THE LITTLE BOOK OF
WREXHAM AFC

MIX
Paper | Supporting
responsible forestry
FSC® C004800

Published in 2023 by OH!

An Imprint of Welbeck Non-Fiction Limited, part of Welbeck Publishing Group.

Offices in London – 20 Mortimer Street, London W1T 3JW
and Sydney – Level 17, 207 Kent St, Sydney NSW 2000 Australia
www.welbeckpublishing.com

Compilation text © Welbeck Non-Fiction Limited 2023
Design © Welbeck Non-Fiction Limited 2023

Disclaimer:

This publication may contain copyrighted material, the use of which has not been specifically authorised by the copyright owner. The material in this publication is made available in this book under the fair use and intended only for review, research and news reporting purposes only. The publisher is not associated with any names, football clubs or associations, trademarks, service marks and trade names referred to herein, which are the property of their respective owners and are used solely for identification purposes. This book is a publication of *OH! an Imprint of Welbeck Non-Fiction Limited* and has not been licensed, approved, sponsored, or endorsed by any person or entity.

All rights reserved. No part of this publication may be reproduced, stored in a retrieval system, or transmitted, in any form or by any means without prior written permission of the publisher, nor be otherwise circulated in any form of binding or cover other than that in which it is published and without a similar condition being imposed on the subsequent purchaser.

A CIP catalogue record of this book is available from the British Library.

ISBN 978 1 80069 616 7

Compiled and written by: Malcolm Croft
Project manager: Russell Porter
Production: Jess Brisley

Printed in Dubai

10 9 8 7 6 5 4 3 2 1

THE LITTLE BOOK OF
WREXHAM
AFC

GENERAL EDITOR: MARK PEARSON

Independent and Unofficial

CONTENTS

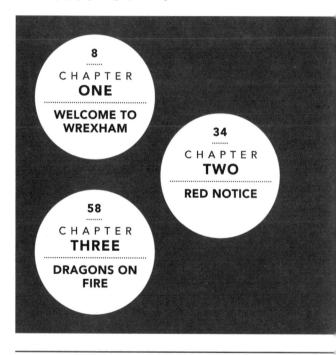

Introduction

After 15 tortuous years of survival and agonising near misses in the fifth tier of English football's national food chain, North Wales' Wrexham AFC did the unthinkable. They actually went up. Their well-deserved promotion in April 2023 – their first in 45 years – became headline news all around the world, thanks to the passion (and funds) of their new owners, Hollywood superheroes Rob McElhenney and Ryan Reynolds. The now-legendary revitalisation of players, management and their loud and proud legion of fans also helped. The 2022/23 season had the whole town*, and the nation, effervescing like a pint of Wrexham Lager.

But the fairy-tale doesn't end there.

For all of Wrexham, and the world-wide audience, the battle to become a team supreme now has to focus on the sequel and face the next challenge – League 2. Can the club stay at the top of their game? Or will relegation return them to the doldrums? Whatever happens next, everyone will be watching Wrexham.

Thankfully, this timely, and tiny, tome of trivia has everything your obsession with the Red Dragons could ever need. It celebrates the wonders of this resilient football club, its people, and the dark secrets that lurk deep inside its long and winding past, present and future. From killer quips to classic quotes, snacky facts to super-sized stats, and lots of other cool things to boot, this compact compendium is the bedside companion every Wrexham fan** deserves as a daily reminder of the club's blockbuster rise to fame, fortune and glory.

Croeso i Wrecsam…

*Technically we're a city now, having attained city status in September 2022. However to all true Wrexham fans we'll always be "the Town".

**Also good as a Christmas present for Chester fans (should you have any as friends!!).

CHAPTER 1

• • •

WELCOME TO WREXHAM

Wrexham's road to superstar status has not always been paved with the gold dust of a thousand ground-down Oscars. The club's future may now have all the hallmarks of a Hollywood movie starring Ryan Reynolds (Indeed, inevitably, the team's 2023 triumph will be made into a meta-movie starring Ryan Reynolds) but its history is full of own goals.

Let's enjoy the rollercoaster ride that was Wrexham's remarkable rise to the top in tasty titbits of trivia…

Up the Town!

On 22 April 2023, Wrexham won their first league title in 45 years, and were promoted to the English Football League Two following that earth-shattering 3–1 win against Boreham Wood.

The first known and recorded settlement in Wrexham was Wristleham Castle, a motte and bailey fortress located on a prehistoric hillfort in (what is now known as) Erddig Park, a National Trust estate.

1882

The year Wrexham Lager Brewery became
the first place in the UK to brew lager beer.
Beer and football have remained best friends
in the town ever since.

"The Lager", as the company is known
locally, have been a long-time sponsor and
have a stand in their name. The history of the
beer and brewery has parallels with the
club, having been rescued from oblivion
several years ago.

Wrexham Lager was the only lager served on the Titanic.*

*Presumably not enjoyed ice-cold.

The ten founding members who represented Wrexham in the club's first ever game at The Racecourse in 1864.

1. Charles Edward Kershaw (Captain)
2. William Tootell
3. Thomas Henry Sykes
4. Thomas Broster
5. Thomas Hanmer
6. Edward Ephraim Knibbs
7. Thomas Heath
8. John Taylor
9. Joseph Roberts
10. George Rumsey Johnston

26 January 1957

On this day Wrexham played an FA Cup fourth-round tie against Manchester United, at home. A record attendance at the Racecourse was set with 34,445 spectators. Wrexham lost 5-nil.

* Wrexham played Manchester United again, in a friendly, on 25 July 2023, in San Diego.

Horse racing was finally abandoned at the Racecourse in 1913.

Pistyll Rhaeadr and Wrexham steeple,
Snowdon's mountain without its people,
Overton yew trees, St. Winifred's Well,
Llangollen's Bridge and Gresford's bells –

The famous rhyme that depicts the
"Seven Wonders of Wales" – three of which
are in Wrexham – St Giles' Church, The
Gresford Bells and the Overton Yew Trees;
and as all are in North Wales we can safely
assume the author was a local writer!

Mullin'ed

A term to explain the unbeatable quality of Paul Mullin, as coined by Luke Garrard, coach of Boreham Wood, when he said his team "simply got Mullin'ed tonight," * following their well-deserved 3-1 loss.

* Ryan Reynolds later joked, "I wouldn't mind getting Mullin'ed."

" That penalty save – I've played over 500 games and I probably had two of those moments in my career – but I've never saved a penalty last minute to win the game. So that just vindicated my decision to carry on playing! The buzz at Wrexham is incredible. **"**

BEN FOSTER

Foster later revealed, "I'm 40 years old and I got cramp in my calf when I made the save... but it was a special moment."

"" Football is a horrible, cyclical, prophetic hellscape that never ceases or ebbs. I love every second, but it's torment in equal measure. **""**

ROB McELHENNEY

❝One thing that is running through my head over and over again is that people said at the beginning, 'Why Wrexham, why Wrexham?' This is exactly why Wrexham.**❞**

RYAN REYNOLDS

On the fans storming the pitch following the 3-1 Boreham Wood victory

The Football Association of Wales (the third oldest football association in the World) was founded in Wrexham in February 1876.

1 December 1883

On this day, Wrexham Athletic Football Club played in the English F.A. Cup for the first time. And last. They were banned after "crowd trouble" caused chaos during a second-round tie against Oswestry, at The Racecourse.

To get around the ban, the club played 1884 tournament under the name Wrexham Olympic Football Club. They remained under that name until 1888 when they became Wrexham FC

Top Ten All Time Goal Scorers

1. Tommy Bamford – 207
2. Arfon Griffiths – 142
3. Karl Connelly – 133
4. Graham Whittle – 117
5. Gary Bennett – 114
6. Ron Hewitt – 111
7. Tommy Bannan – 100
8. Albert Kinsey – 99
9. Billy Ashcroft – 96
10. Andy Morrell – 92

"With Wrexham it's more that I can see what it means to the supporters. They've been through such hard times, to give them this back is unbelievable. Wrexham's supporters literally had to buy the club to keep it from going bankrupt. When you see people putting their mortgages up for a football club, and then you represent that football club, you really have to give it your all.**"**

PAUL MULLIN

"Everybody knows it's a difficult journey we've got ahead of us but if we don't have ambition and if we don't have time, then ultimately why do we do this? If actually Rob and Ryan are doing this, the key is they want to deliver a community benefit to the people of Wrexham. If they can do that via the football club, which is gaining global accolades, then the biggest beneficiaries are the people of Wrexham.**"**

SHAUN HARVEY

Advisor to the Board

Welsh Your Mouth Out

Phrases every Wrexham fan will know:

Cymru – Wales

Sut mae? – How are you?

Pob lwc – Good luck

Iechyd Da – cheers

Diolch – thanks

Da Iawn – very good

Os gwelwch yn dda – please!

Llongyfarchiadau – congratulations

Cwrw – beer

Pencampwyr – champions

Wrexham Superheroes

The 27-man team that delivered the
League Two promotion. Heroes, one and all.

1 – Rob Lainton / Ben Foster (for 8 games)
2 – Reece Hall-Johnson
3 – Callum McFadzean
4 – Ben Tozer
5 – Aaron Hayden
6 – Jordan Tunnicliffe

7 – Jordan Davies	21 – Mark Howard
8 – Luke Young	22 – Tom O'Connor
9 – Ollie Palmer	25 – Ryan Austin
10 – Paul Mullin	26 – Harry Lennon
11 – Liam McAlinden	27 – Jake Bickerstaff
13 – Christian Dibble	30 – James Jones
14 – Anthony Forde	32 – Max Cleworth
17 – Bryce Hosannah	33 – Dan Jones
19 – Jake Hyde	37 – Kai Evans
20 – Dior Angus	38 – Elliot Lee

1 April 2023

Wrexham's 5-1 walloping of Oldham Athletic was no April Fools.

In fact, it was the first time in history the club crossed the 100-league point threshold.

404%

The percentage turnover increase in the first full season of Rob and Ryan's ownership, according to The Athletic. The club achieved £6 million in turnover, a record.

However, the club posted a loss of £2.9 million in 2021/2022 season

2022/2023 Top Goal Scorers

	Player	Goals	Shot Accuracy*
1.	Paul Mullin	46	91 per cent
2.	Ollie Palmer	16	94 per cent
3.	Elliot Lee	14	93 per cent
4.	Aaron Hayden	11	85 per cent
5.	Sam Dalby	8	82 per cent
6.	Thomas O'Connor	6	70 per cent
7.	James Jones	5	83 per cent
8.	Jacob Mendy	4	100 per cent
9.	Ben Tozer	4	100 per cent
10.	Jordan Davies	3	100 per cent

Data from the BBC

❝It will probably go down in Wrexham's history and being a local lad as part of the squad that got us promoted after so many years, it would mean the world to me.❞

JORDAN DAVIES

Wrexham's midfielder speaking before promotion. Davies was the only player in the 2022/2023 squad born in Wrexham or more precisely Coedpoeth, hence his nickname the Coedy Assassin

CHAPTER 2

• • •

RED NOTICE

The colour red seems to follow Ryan Reynolds around. From the Red Dragons to the colour of his superhero suit in *Deadpool*, it's always there.

There's also been many a red flag, red card, red tape, and red notices of bankruptcy and eviction in Wrexham's dark history too, with many fans seething red with rage in bad times, and painting the town red in the good times.

Secrets and revelations of Wrexham's desperate 150-year fight for survival will be revealed within this chapter!

"The ambition of the club attracted me here; it was something I really wanted to be a part of.**"**

PAUL MULLIN

" The biggest challenge was the community going 'What the fuck are these two guys doing here?' **"**

RYAN REYNOLDS

2026

The year Wales's National Football Museum
will open – in Wrexham.

The city was chosen not just because of
its current popularity but it was where the
Football Association of Wales (FAW)
was formed in 1876 at a meeting in the
Wynnstay Arms.

89%

The increase, in comparison to this time last
year, in property searches in Wrexham,
according to GetAgent, in April 2023,
following the club's promotion.
The research also revealed that searches
for "buy a house in Wrexham" are also up
75% year on year.

"We know how much people in this town wanted to get back in the Football League, how much they wanted to experience Football League life again and the sense of pride that comes with that.**"**

HUMPHREY KER

£2.09

In August 2022, a survey revealed that the cheapest location for a pint in the UK can be found in Wrexham, where the average cost of a pint is £2.09 – almost £4 cheaper than the nation's most expensive pint, in London.

❝ Much good, some ill, he did;
so hope all's even. **❞**

TOMB INSCRIPTION

*Head to Wrexham's 800-year-old St Giles' Church, one of the Seven
Wonders of Wales, to find the tombstone of Elihu Yale, who founded
America's prestigious Yale University, Connecticut, in 1701*

“Rob's telling me how the show
Sunderland Until I Die had him in tears one
minute, then jumping out of his seat the next.
But then he says, 'We should do this.
Buy a football team. But do it in reverse, by
buying a club already struggling and try
to turn it around'.**”**

HUMPHREY KER

100 million

The number of U.S. households that watched at least one Wrexham game in the 2022/2023 season, as revealed by ESPN.

> **"** Ryan's obsession with Wrexham, and all of Wales, is becoming problematic. I'm trying to get us ready to shoot *Deadpool 3* and he's so distracted by this football team. I need to downgrade his obsession a bit, because he can't get any work done. **"**

SHAUN LEVY

Director of Deadpool 3

"Wrexham is absolutely thriving. The documentary has had a huge impact on dozens of local businesses. Results on the pitch are helping because it is bringing in lots more people, spending money. Everyone seems to be buying in to it, thanks to Ryan and Rob.**"**

WAYNE JONES

Owner of The Turf pub

£8 million

The club's estimated value in 2023. This marks a 400 per cent increase on Ryan and Rob's initial two million investment.

74%

Overall percentage of league games won in 2022-23 season. Just seven per cent defeat – that's three games. League average was 37 per cent.

2022-2023 Season Totals

116 goals scored

111 league points

46 games played

34 games won

9 draws

3 losses

Two criteria

Rob and Ryan had never met each other before purchasing the club. McElhenney only got the idea to buy a club after watching the documentary *Sunderland 'Til I Die* after having run out of TV to watch during lockdown.

In Rob's mind, two criteria were essential: Supporter-owned and debt-free.

Wrexham was the one.

2.52

Average number of goals
per game scored over 46 games in
the 2022-2023 season.

Wrexham's wage bill for players is
believed to be seven times higher than
that of other National League teams,
working out a total across all players at
£3,616,080 in 2022.

"Reynolds and McElhenney are so passionate about the club — and the community. I see a lot of it off-camera: how much they're enjoying it, how much they're invested in it — not just financially but emotionally. It's genuine. And the football club deserves this. They've endured a lot of hardship. They deserve every bit of what's going on right now.**"**

OLLIE PALMER

❝As I've told Rob and Ryan from the start, there will come a time where we're in the Championship and we draw three games in a row, and one of you will get called a cunt in Manchester Airport by a Wrexham fan. Eventually, the most valuable story in football will be their comeuppance, it'll be their downfall. But that's just part of life and we'll come to it when it arrives.**❞**

HUMPHREY KER

2022 FA Trophy

On 22 May, for the first time in seven years
Wrexham played in the final of the FA Trophy.

They were beaten at Wembley Stadium
by Bromley by one measly goal. More than
45,000 fans turned up.

" I wish I'd thought of that. **"**

RYAN REYNOLDS

Commenting after a large Hollywood-style sign that read
WREXHAM in large white letters was installed on Bersham Bank,
overlooking the A483, August 2022

Sing When You Win No.1

❝We've got Mullin, Super Paul Mullin,
I don't quite think you understand.
He plays in red and white,
He's fucking dynamite,
We've got super Paul Mullin!**❞**

TERRACE CHANT
for Rob and Ryan's first super signing, the one and only, Paul Mullin

• • •

CHAPTER 3

DRAGONS ON FIRE

The last few years have seen the
Red Dragons emerge victorious on
many occasions, taking the fans
back to former glory days.

This chapter dives down into
all the good things the club
is doing right. Time to celebrate
with wit, wisdom and a
whole lot of Wrexham…

"We didn't know anything about the sport – now we're obsessed with it. Now I love this sport so much that I hate it. It's a living, breathing, screaming nightmare for me. It's one of the greatest things that's ever happened to me and genuinely one of the worst.**"**

RYAN REYNOLDS

❝I will admit to you that when Ryan bought Wrexham, I did get more than one offer from rivals to that team for one pound to come in as a co-owner.**❞**

HUGH JACKMAN

Ryan's faux foe

❝When I get my hands on Ben Foster, he's gonna be on the injured list because I'm gonna break ribs I'm gonna hug him so hard. ❞

RYAN REYNOLDS

About Ben Foster, after that penalty save

" There's The Turf and my customers are my life. I live and breathe it, it's my dream job. **"**

WAYNE JONES

Owner of the Turf pub

❝We have an inquiry from AFC Wrexham. Just got a call from their new owners, showbiz magnates Rob McElhenney and Ryan Reynolds. I can't tell if them buying the club is a joke or not, so I haven't replied to them yet.**❞**

HIGGINS

Ted Lasso

❝The Disney+ documentary was probably 10 times better for the audience because we lost in season one. I got loads of texts from friends of mine, saying how the show blew their minds only to then be shocked at the end because we lost. They hadn't expected that. But we are not *Ted Lasso*. This is real life. You can't choose your ending.**❞**

HUMPHREY KER

"There is one thing, gentlemen. I wish to name, the great want of amusement in this town in winter time. It is my intention to purchase a football in the course of this week, and I shall expect a good many down to the field next Saturday."

EDWARD MANNERS

The cricket club chairman at the end of season dinner in The Turf Tavern, 4 October 1864 (the day Wrexham turned into a footballing town)

1864

Wrexham was founded, making it
the oldest football club in Wales and the third
oldest professional club in the world.

In the same year, Abraham Lincoln
had just been re-elected as president amidst
America's Civil War.

Fellow-promoted club Notts County are the oldest.

Mission Statement

"We will reward the faith of the supporters who have stood by Wrexham AFC through its history by putting everything we have towards what all fans want most for their club, and that is to... WIN, WIN, WIN."

Rob McElhenney and Ryan Reynolds

"Hi, I'm Will Ferrell. It's my first time here – where are we again? Wrexham! I'm really excited for this match and I'll be honest with you, I'm a little nervous.**"**

WILL FERRELL

1877

The year that Wrexham's club ground,
The Racecourse, began its tenure as the
oldest international stadium still in use in the
world. The 10,500-capacity site hosted
Wales's first home international game.
They lost to Scotland.

The most recent international home game
played here was Wales men's team against
Trinidad and Tobago in March 2019.

£100,000

The figure raised, on 11 August 2011,
in just seven hours by Wrexham fans to save
the club from expulsion from the National
League due to unpaid tax bill of £200,000.

From this point, the Wrexham
Supporters Trust (WST) took full control of
the club. One fan even handed over the
deeds of his house.

2007/2008 season

After finishing bottom in League Two,
Wrexham were relegated to the National
League – the first time they had played non-
league football in 88 years.

" People were turning up from all corners of North Wales to give their life savings to save Wrexham AFC says it all about the passion the fans have for the club… Whichever way you look at it, it was a monumental day. With everything going on with the club now, the documentary etc, that day is precisely why it is an underdog story - there would be no story now being told if it wasn't for what the fans did that day. **"**

TIM EDWARDS

Wrexham Fan

22 October 1864

The date of Wrexham's first ever game was played two weeks after Wrexham Cricket Club announced they wanted to form their own football team as activity for the winter months. Over a pint (or two) in the Turf Hotel, Wrexham A.F.C. was born.

The squad was called Wrexham Football and Athletic Club and played against the Prince of Wales Fire Brigade. Both sides could only muster 10 players. The Fire Brigade won 2-1.

96

The minute in extra time when former retired Man Utd. goalkeeper, Ben Foster, saved Notts County's Cedwyn Scott's penalty kick to ensure Wrexham won 3-2.

Sing When You Win No.2

❝We are Wrexham FC
We're never gonna die
Unlike our Chester neighbours
Who kissed their club goodbye
We're going for promotion
We're shagging all the sheep
(shagging all the sheep)
We are Wrexham FC
We're gonna win the league!**❞**

TERRACE CHANT

❝Our intention is to become part of the Wrexham story rather than Wrexham becoming part of our story. **❞**

RYAN REYNOLDS

13 Salisbury Road

The Wrexham address of Hollywood actor, Russell Crowe's great grandfather, Frederick William Crowe, who lived in the town until 1925 before emigrating to Canada with his 12 children.

❝Go on Wrexham! Lifting hearts and trophies. If you don't yet know what the two R's have been up to. It's a great story so far, and it's only just begun.**❞**

RUSSELL CROWE

Commenting on the promotion

❝It was my birthday. I was out of work at the time, I'd recently been made redundant. I had £500 to my name and I took it all out, walked up to the ground and handed it over. There were kids there emptying their piggy banks and handing over their pocket money, it was unbelievable.**❞**

RICHARD ULRICH

Wrexham Fan and WST member

22 April 2023

The day of the final league match of the season versus Boreham Wood – the Turf Pub was forced to shut its doors for the first time in 15 years.

More than 150 punters queued nine hours outside the pub before kick-off to ensure a spot in the bar.

In October 2022, Paul Mullin was banned
from wearing boots bearing the slogan,
"Fuck the Tories!"

After the team's 3-1 win against
Boreham Wood, video emerged on
YouTube of Mullin and assorted customers
singing "Fuck the Tories!" in the local
McDonalds late at 2am.

❝Mr Speaker, can I join my right honourable friend in congratulating everyone at Wrexham, from the owners to the players to the supporters and everyone in the community, it's been an incredible ride, we've all enjoyed watching them and we wish them every future success, Mr Speaker, and they are indeed a jewel in the crown and she deserves enormous credit for championing them in this place.**❞**

RISHI SUNAK

The British Prime Minister, speaking in the Houses of Parliament

❝Just a quick note to thank each and every one of you on our one-year anniversary with the club. The love and adoration for Wrexham FC – it's unlike anything we've ever seen.That's why we've put up 365 Aviation Gin and Tonics behind the bar. Have one on us. Cheers.**❞**

ROB AND RYAN

1-0

The final score Wrexham Women needed to secure promotion to the Welsh top-flight and an historic semi-professional status as they defeated Briton Ferry 1-0 in the promotion play-off final.

❝This is the third-oldest club on the planet and we don't see why it can't have a global appeal.**❞**

RYAN REYNOLDS

“We've had to shut. They've completely drank us dry. It was bonkers, we had probably 450 people outside, and God knows how many hundreds inside – we were up to capacity in both. We've actually shut for the first time in 15 years!**”**

WAYNE JONES

98.6%

On September 23, 2020, 2,000 members of the Wrexham Supporters Trust (WST) voted overwhelmingly to allow Rob McElhenney and Ryan Reynolds takeover of the club.

Before the purchase by Rob and Ryan, the number of Wrexham's TikTok followers was zero.

In May 2023, it was 1.3 million.

And TikTok were the proud club sponsor for both 2021/22 and the promotion season.

Sing When You Win No.3

❝Oh, Parky do you know what he's worth.
Ollie Palmer's the best on earth.
A lanky striker is just what we need.
Taking Wrexham to the football league.❞

TERRACE CHANT

Club Captain Ben Tozer played every single minute of the club's 2022/2023 season.

He also scored four goals.

"On Saturday last a football match was played on the ground at the Turf Tavern, between ten of the Prince of Wales Fire Brigade and ten of the club, which resulted in an easy victory for the fire brigade, they winning the first two goals out of three.**"**

WREXHAM ADVERTISER

The team's first ever review, 29 October 1864

"I never got to play for my beloved club, so seeing the company name on the shirts was the next best thing! **"**

PHIL SALMON

Former shirt sponsor and Wrexham Supporters Trust Board member, Phil of AEC Engineering, overrating his footballing prowess (with tongue in cheek - we think!). However he was one of the many fans whose support of the club throughout the dark times kept Wrexham FC alive

• • •

CHAPTER 4

WROB AND WRYAN

The real Princes of Wales are, of course, the two new owners of the club, Rob McElhenney and Ryan Reynolds.

Without their involvement, investment, and imagination, none of Wrexham's inspiration on, and off, the pitch would have happened.

To quote our favourite song, "Bring on the Deadpool and Rob McElhenney!" – the superstar saviours of Wrexham AFC.

❝Your average five-year-old in Wrexham has forgotten more about football than we will ever know. **❞**

RYAN REYNOLDS

" Llanfairpwllgwyn-
gyllgogerychwyrndrobwllllantysilio-
gogogoch. **"**

ROB McELHENNEY

The longest place name in the UK, expertly pronounced by Rob
in the Welcome to Wrexham *documentary*

❝This is against one of our main rivals from our first season as co-chairmen of the club. Stockport County got promoted over us last season. We're still a little bit bitter about that but feel free to deliver Stockport County 31 flavours of humiliation. Don't hold back.**❞**

ROB AND RYAN

FIFA 23

“Paul Mullin is one of
the greatest footballers in the world. **”**

ROB McELHENNEY

During the airing of Season One
of *Welcome to Wrexham*, the club's online
shop quadrupled in sales, with a total
value of £290,170.

In the same period a year earlier, the
club made £59,674.

12 miles

The distance of dual carriageway that separates Wrexham from the posh city of their arch rivals, the English team, Chester FC, and home to the abysmal, adolescent TV soap opera, *Hollyoaks*.

What more do you need to know to need never go?

"There's not a second of any day of the week when I don't think 'Those poor people of Wrexham. That poor town. That poor football team. I'm so sorry for you. I did one movie with Ryan 20 years ago. I cannot get him out of my life. Trust me, get him out!**"**

HUGH JACKMAN

❝I'm in a puddle of happy tears and covered in chill bumps. I am in love with Wrexham and... you.**❞**

HUGH JACKMAN

Tweet to Reynolds after watching the documentary

Welsh Songs to sing at the ground!

Mae hen wlad fy nhaddau – Land of my
fathers (Welsh National Anthem)
Yma o hyd – We're still here. Sung before
every game

And traditional tunes "appropriated"
Wrexham is the Name – to the tune of *Men of
Harlech*
Wrexham Lager, Wrexham Lager – to the tune
of *Bread of Heaven*

14

The number of times Wrexham and Notts County swapped the top position of the National League in the 2022/2023 season. Wrexham secured the No.1 spot for the last time in their 3-2 victory against Notts County on April 10.

Sing When You Win No.4

"I saw my mate the other day…
he said he'd seen the white Pele
So I asked, "who is he?"
He goes by the name of Elliot Lee
Elliot Lee, Elliot Lee
Goes by the name of Elliot Lee.**"**

TERRACE CHANT

12

The number of times Wrexham went a
goal down in games during the 2022/2023
season. Wrexham went on to win seven of
these games, a tally unmatched by any other
National League team.

The Robins

Today, Wrexham are famously known as the Red Dragons. However, that name only came about in 2001.

From the 1900s, the team were known as "The Robins", after Ted Robinson, who managed the team from 1912 to 1924.

WREX

Wrexham's club mascot is
Wrex the Dragon.

Wrex wears a red dragon head and
the team's home kit with the number
1864, representing the year of the
club's establishment.

The Cornovii tribe of Celtic Britons were the first to settle in Wrexham for several generations before the Romans invaded Britain in 43 AD.

1161

The earliest recorded name of Wrexham
was written as 'Wristleham'.

In 1291 the name was written as 'Gwregsam'
(the G was silent.).

"We had a lovely hug.
Not a bad-looking woman at 77.**"**

BEN TOZER

Captain Tozer's words about Ryan Reynolds' mum

"Get promoted and I'll make you my new stepdad, Tozer!"**"**

RYAN REYNOLDS

Tweet to Ben

❝I was expecting to drink but I wasn't expecting to do multiple shots of gin, which is exactly what we did. **❞**

RYAN REYNOLDS

The first time Rob and Ryan visited The Turf they expected to introduce themselves to owner, Wayne Jones, and fans, over a quick pint. It ended up turning into a drinking session that lasted two days

❝I can't believe there was a time when I thought football was boring.**❞**

ROB McELHENNEY

❝You're now an honorary
Welsh boyo **❞**

ANTHONY HOPKINS

To Ryan Reynolds, after the promotion

"We can feel what it means to the town. This is a moment of catharsis for them and celebration. For us to be welcomed into the community, and to be welcomed into this experience, has been the honour of my life.**"**

ROB MCELHENNEY

" There's something crazy going on here. The documentary is a huge part of it, but I do truly think we're starting to build a momentum and interest that will go beyond that. At some stage the documentary will go away. It's not going to run for 10, 15 years. But we're confident that with the grounding we're putting in place now, the legions of new fans that we have will stick around. **"**

HUMPHREY KER

In April 2023, Wrexham Women's were crowned champions of the Adran League North winning all 12 of their games, scoring 70 goals and conceding just six.

They secured promotion to the highest tier, the Adran Premier, after victory over Briton Ferry, the Adran League South champions.

Gor-au Chwar-ae, Cyd Chwar-ae

The motto of the Football Association of Wales. Translated as 'Team Play is the Best Play'.

"Ollie Palmer is always the first guy that walks out of that dressing room completely shirtless to have a conversation with my wife. I'm like 'Ollie put a fucking shirt on and come back out to speak to her like a gentleman'.**"**

RYAN REYNOLDS

About Ollie Palmer

❝The dressing room is filled with people whose integrity matches their abilities on the field. **❞**

RYAN REYNOLDS

Wrexham is no longer the black sheep of the family. It's now the GOAT.

According to 2019 Welsh government statistics, Wrexham was home to 129,644 sheep and lambs. The population of Wrexham in the same year was almost identical – 135,957, or approx. one sheep per person.

"A little earlier today, I had the opportunity to see one of the other wonders of Wrexham, namely the football club, which is busy putting Wrexham on the map as never before.**"**

KING CHARLES III

❝I'm still somewhere between giggling
and sobbing. This town and this sport
is one of the most romantic things on Earth.
Thank you, Wrexham AFC. **❞**

RYAN REYNOLDS

• • •

CHAPTER 5

MAXIMUM EFFORT

Rob and Ryan may have brought Wrexham back from the brink of extinction, but the promotion to League Two has been a real team effort, involving more funny characters than an episode of *It's Always Sunny*.

From superstar signings to grand ambitions, dumb luck to lots of blood, sweat and tears, the 2022/2023 seasons was stuffed full of maximum effort, the catchphrase of Mr Deadpool himself.

These are the real superheroes of Wrexham… capes not included.

"Maybe we don't make it all the way to the Premier League. But if this club is promoted, once, twice, that's epic, right? That's history.**"**

RYAN REYNOLDS

❝ I think I speak for a lot of the lads when I say, these two owners are successful in their business, they're famous all over the world… but they're in football now. And if they want to be successful in football, it doesn't matter what's gone before. It's still footie, isn't it? **❞**

PAUL MULLIN

❝Like someone boiled you both down and poured the results into a mould.**❞**

HUMPHREY KER

On the fact that Ollie Palmer looks like a cross between
Ryan and Rob

Giant Killers

Wrexham are accomplished Cup giant killers,
having defeated several top-tier clubs.

1974 – Southampton 0, Wrexham 1

1976 – Tottenham Hotspur 2, Wrexham 3

1981 – Wrexham 1, West Ham 0

1991 – Wrexham 2, Arsenal 1 (then Premier League
champions!)

1995– Wrexham 2, Ipswich Town 1

1997 – West Ham 0, Wrexham 1

1999 – Wrexham 2, Middlesbrough 1

2023 – Coventry 3, Wrexham 4

And in Europe

1984 Wrexham 1, FC Porto 0 (agg 4-4 Wrexham win
on away goals)

" When I was at Wimbledon, I'd chat to the lads and say: 'Lads, if I'm not having a barbeque with Ryan Reynolds in the summer and playing two touch with him then something has gone wrong!' And lo and behold he's just invited me for a barbeque. **"**

OLLIE PALMER

Eight miles from Wrexham is the Pontcysyllte Aqueduct, the longest, highest and most famous aqueduct in Britain. It stands at 39m high above the River Dee and is 11 miles long.

In 2009, it was inscribed as a UNESCO World Heritage Site. It took 10 years to build, starting 1795.

Sing When You Win No.5

"We've got super Phil Parky
He knows exactly what we need
Tozer at the back
Mullin in attack
Taking Wrexham to the football league.**"**

TERRACE CHANT

3,111%

The increase in percentage of followers gained on Wrexham's Instagram account since news of Rob and Ryan's purchase was announced.

❝So many things that have happened
that if you wrote it for a movie, it would
sound far-fetched. **❞**

OLLIE PALMER

"Iron-Mad" John Wilkinson, the English industrialist who pioneered the manufacture of cast iron, kickstarted the Industrial Revolution in Wrexham with the opening of the Bersham Ironworks. Here, Wilkinson invented a precision boring machine, the first in the world to make cannons and steam engine cylinders. It is regarded as the first ever machine tool.

Friday, 22 September 1934

The Gresford Colliery Disaster is known as the city's darkest day.

The UK's worst coal mining disaster caused the loss of 266 lives at 2.08am when a violent explosion rippled through the mine starting an underground fire.

Only 11 bodies were recovered.

Many of the miners working had doubled their shift so that they could watch the Wrexham-Tranmere match the next day.

The date is commemorated each year by the club and the year 1934 is incorporated into the team shirt design

£4,800

Paul Mullin's weekly salary.

This is nearly x5 times more than the average weekly wage at National League level, estimated at £1,000.

"We've had board meetings where
Rob and Ryan said they want to
do this until they're 70. Initially the idea was
to do five to 10 years and see where we
got to after that. But I think they are addicted
to it now. **"**

HUMPHREY KER

❝I was sat in the house and got a phone call from Rob McElhenney while sat in my mum's garden. It came up as Beverly Hills and I was like 'That's alright, aint it'. At that point, I wasn't thinking I was going to sign for Wrexham. But when I got off the phone with him, I could feel his passion and what they wanted to do with the club…

He made it very clear they wanted to be successful and they were going to do everything they could to get there. Now, I'm so grateful I've done it. 🔗

PAUL MULLIN

❝I thought it would be a lot of fun and there are aspects of the endeavour that have been incredibly fun, life-alteringly fun, but it is definitely not fun to watch a football match. Every Saturday morning is absolute misery in my house until I hear that final whistle. I just can't believe how it's gripped my entire nervous system.**❞**

ROB McELHENNEY

If they had bought another club
in this league, it wouldn't be the same.
It's the fans and the city as a whole
which makes it so exciting. **"**

OLLIE PALMER

In the 2022/2023 season, Wrexham won 22 of their 23 home matches, another club record smashed.

The only match getting in the way of a 100% record was the 2-2 draw with Woking.

FA Cup

In 2022, Wrexham reached the final 32 teams (out of 732!) of the FA Cup, and the only remaining non-league team in the country.

They were beaten by Sheffield United 3-1 in the Fourth Round replay after a 3-3 draw at the Racecourse.

"We'd never met physically. I admired Rob for what he'd accomplished and built in the television world. I remember once seeing an episode of *Sunny* that blew me away and I slid into his DMs to tell him.**"**

RYAN REYNOLDS

On how he met Rob

" We're two people who've made a career of never taking ourselves too seriously. However, we realize taking stewardship of this great and storied club is an incredibly serious matter and something we don't take lightly. **"**

ROB AND RYAN

• • •

CHAPTER 6

IT'S ALWAYS SUNNY IN WREXHAM

With promotion secured and faith in the club restored, all is sunny in Wrexham.

Before the hard work starts in the second act of the club's comeback, let's kick off our boots and take a moment to relish all that has happened in the crazy first few years of this new millennium.

From relegation to promotion, Hollywood to Rhosllanerchrugog, this story is only getting started. The only way is up, right?

"You're watching games for the better part of a year on a shitty YouTube feed. Then you walk in here. The place is bigger than it looked onscreen, and I mean that figuratively. You feel a history, a legacy that's woven into the stands and the rusting bars.**"**

RYAN REYNOLDS

152

❝I tend to go zero to 10. Abject despair when we go 1-0 down. Then we score and I'm, like, 'WE MIGHT GET PROMOTED TO THE PREMIER LEAGUE IN FOUR YEARS.'**❞**

ROB McELHENNEY

"A huge reason Rob wanted to do this in the first place was to find somewhere that was deserving of some good news and a good time. I think he gave them that.**"**

HUMPHREY KER

"When you've got owners on top like Rob and Ryan, you want to run through more bricks for them. So, from a playing point of view, it definitely helps the players. But, also, I see them as completely normal people now.**"**

OLLIE PALMER

❝I saw somebody resilient.
And those are the people you want to
spend your life working with.
Also, I had TV money, but I needed
superhero movie money.**❞**

ROB McELHENNEY

On why he chose Ryan Reynolds as co-chairman.

Wrexham Winning Honours

1977/78 –Third Division (3rd level) –
Champions

2012/13 – FA Trophy Winners

2004/05 – Football League Trophy Winners

1997/98, 1999/00, 2000/01, 2002/03 &
2003/04 – FAW Premier Cup Winners

1877–1985 – Welsh Cup Winners – 23 times
(national record)

❝I love every second of hating it. Wrexham AFC is the greatest drug on earth. **❞**

RYAN REYNOLDS

" The toughest, gruffest, coal mining guy
told me, 'If you're born in Wales,
you're born with the fist of a fighter and the
heart of a poet'. That felt like beauty to me.
That felt like the kind of culture I would
want to foster and cultivate at a football club.
And it turns out that there's not only a
whole town that embodies that but an
entire nation that does. **"**

ROB McELHENNEY

❝Players and staff have performed to give the fans what they've wanted for 15 years – promotion to the Football League.
I'm over the moon for the people of the town, they've taken to me like I was born here.
I love it here. To repay them tonight with this promotion is unbelievable. I'm looking forward to a season in League Two now.**❞**

PAUL MULLIN

“You see a direct connection with the people of Wrexham to the people of Philadelphia because the club is the beating heart of the community and that's exactly what we see here in Philadelphia.**”**

ROB McELHENNEY

The Philadelphia Eagles won their first ever Super Bowl in 2018.
The victory shocked the world. A native Philadelphian, the win inspired Rob
and he saw a parallel with Wrexham – a team that deserves more for a
city that is devoted to football

'It's Always Sunny in Wrexham'

The now-iconic song written by Declan Swans' Michael 'Scoot' Hett, 'It's Always Sunny in Wrexham' has become a huge hit for the comedy indie band.

The chorus's line of, "No-one's invested so much as a penny / Bring on the Deadpool and Rob McElhenney!" will be a terrace chant for generations to come. Indeed, Rob wants it played at his funeral, he said.

" People know we've been 15 years outside the league and the journey the club has been on in that time. It has been torturous at times with the club nearly going out of business. But what the owners have done, the positivity in the town about the football club, and how people have galvanised that has been very special. **"**

PHIL PARKINSON

❝The bars were too busy so we ended up going back to the stadium as a team. At 6am I went to the medical room to try and kip on one of the physiotherapy beds. Then at 6.20am the physio comes in singing 'We've got Mullin, super Paul Mullin' he wakes me up. Then we're out again. I was awake for 40 hours. People were hanging off lampshades at one point.**❞**

PAUL MULLIN

On the celebrations after promotion was confirmed

Alexander Hamilton

The name now and forever despised by Wrexham fans. It was Hamilton who, in 2002, began Wrexham's 21st century problems, including cancelling the club's Racecourse lease, racking up large unpaid tax bills, mismanaging and exploiting the club for his own gain and asset-stripping.

In 2010, a judge banned him for being a company director for seven years.

19 May 2022

Wrexham Lager won the 'Best beer from the UK' (for their Wrexham Lager Export 330ml bottle), award at the Frankfurt International Beer Trophy, one of the largest beer competitions.

"I want to be excited about playing football every day, and what more exciting place are you going to find than Wrexham? Every week something exciting happens.**"**

PAUL MULLIN

"*Deadpool 3* is around the corner, maybe we'll get a shout in that, never know.**"**

PAUL MULLIN

In 2011, Wrexham was completely owned by its supporters, the WST.

At the time Rob and Ryan began showing interest in the club, it had sunk to its lowest position in the league in 150 years.

ff This is the third oldest professional football club on Earth that plays in the oldest international stadium on earth. It is serious business to each and every person.
I don't care whether you're five years old in Wrexham or you're 95 years old. There is a passion. **jj**

RYAN REYNOLDS

Cross-border Derby
Wrexham vs. Chester FC

The last time they played arch-rivals,
Chester FC, in March 2018 Wrexham won
the game 2-0. They have played each other
146 times. Wrexham has won the most.
Chester were relegated from the National
League at the end of the 2017–18 season.

The teams first played each other
on 8 December 1888. Wrexham won 3-2.

❝ We want to reach a point where we're not reliant on the guys reaching into their pockets. We'll never lose the Rob and Ryan effect, that will be there always. But we need to plan for life without the documentary and all the attention that comes with that. **❞**

HUMPHREY KER

❝One of the reasons the owners bought the club was because of the huge potential and the history of the club. It is too long for a club of this stature and this catchment area and potential to be out of the league but no one is going to hand it to us. We are going to have to work incredibly hard to be at the top of the league and the work started on the first day of pre-season.**❞**

PHIL PARKINSON

Division Costs

As Wrexham rise up through the leagues
so too will their value:

Division	Value (£)	Value ($)
Premier League	214.6 – 925.5 m	266.9 m – 1.15 billion
Championship	17.9 – 115.9 m	22.2 – 144.1 m
League One	5.2 – 17.19 m	6.5 – 21.4 m
League Two	3 – 9 m	3.7 – 11.2 m

as per transfermarkt.com figures

*A League Two has more than five times as much financial value than
Wrexham. Premier League clubs, such as Manchester United, are valued at
more than £5 billion*

"Everything I own smells like champagne, beer and grass. I'm still somewhere between giggling and sobbing. This town and this sport is one of the most romantic things on earth."

RYAN REYNOLDS

£2 million ($2.5 million)

The suspected amount that Ryan and Rob
bought Wrexham in 2021.

On 9 December 2022, former Prince of Wales, King Charles III, and Queen Consort Camilla, visited The Racecourse and introduced themselves to the new princes of Wales, Rob and Ryan.

The King was overheard joking with head groundsman Paul Chaloner, saying:

❝It is proper grass isn't it, not that plastic stuff?.**❞**

The new pitch was the first big headache of the new owners, costing £300,000 in 2021

177

"Back in February 2021, when we first became custodians of the Club, it was identified that reverting the Racecourse Ground to a four-sided stadium was a priority for us.**"**

ROB AND RYAN

1 June 2023

Construction began on the brand new 5,500-seater Kop stand at Wrexham's Racecourse Ground, following a grant of £25million from the Welsh government.

It is expected to be complete ahead of the 2024/25 season.

Wrexham Players of the Year

1. 2012–13 – Chris Westwood
2. 2013–14 – Mark Carrington
3. 2014–15 – Manny Smith
4. 2015–16 – Connor Jennings
5. 2016–17 – Martin Riley
6. 2017–18 – Shaun Pearson
7. 2018–19 – Rob Lainton
8. 2019–20 – Luke Young
9. 2020–21 – Luke Young
10. 2021–22 – Paul Mullin

10 – 1

Wrexham's best ever league win.
Against Hartlepool United, 3 March 1962.

❝There is a lot of work going on behind the scenes with the infrastructure of the club and the owners are trying to build a club for the long term. The aim in the short term is to try and start the season well and get to the top of the league. Every game is going to be like a cup tie and we've got to be ready to play in that cup-tie manner.**❞**

PHIL PARKINSON

"Wages-wise, it's literally peanuts…
the part for me is getting the team
over the line and getting them promoted.
I'm a very low maintenance player. Just
wheel me out, I'll do a job. **"**

BEN FOSTER

"I feel this is a squad which can take the club forward for a few years to come. There is talent in the squad. There are players who are only going to get better, there is a good blend of experience and youth.**"**

PHIL PARKINSON

During the 2022/2023 season, players were awarded an extra £200 for each win and £50 for a draw, as long as Wrexham remain in a play-off position.

A further £250,000 bonus pot was awarded to all players upon promotion, alongside an all-expenses paid "party trip" to Las Vegas.

RR McReynolds

The actual owner of Wrexham is a fictional person, or rather a smashing together of the two co-chairmen, Ryan Reynolds and Rob McElhenney.

On 27–28 May 2023, America's coolest
20-million-selling rock band, the Kings of
Leon, performed at the Racecourse.

Their support band was… drum roll
please… Declan Swans!

Crowd chants of "Wrexham on Fire" could
be heard during the song, 'Sex on Fire'.

Seeing Red

The Red Dragons have been shown
the red card 211 times in 111-years of
record-keeping.

Steve Buxton remains the player with the
most – he saw red seven times.

In the 2022/2023 the first and only
red card of the season was awarded
to Phil Parkinson for his now infamous
"cheating" spat with Barnet goalkeeper,
Laurie Walker.

116

The number of goals scored by Wrexham
in the 2022/2023 season, across 46 games.
74 at home, 42 away.

Paul Mullin scored 36 in total.

"In 10 years' time, the plan has and always will be the Premier League. If it's theoretically possible to go from the fifth tier to the Premier League, why wouldn't we try?**"**

RYAN REYNOLDS

❝Wrexham AFC is only in a position to thrive because of the incredible efforts of the Wrexham Supporters Trust. Their members are a fitting reflection of the integrity and spirit of the town and they will always have an important role at the club.**❞**

ROB AND RYAN